Under the Sunday Tree

Under the Sunday Tree

Paintings by Mr. Amos Ferguson

Poems by Eloise Greenfield

HARPER & ROW, PUBLISHERS

I am grateful for the support of the
National Endowment for the Arts in Washington, D.C.,
a Federal Agency, and the D.C. Commission
on the Arts and Humanities.

E.G.

Under the Sunday Tree
Paintings copyright © 1988 by Amos Ferguson
Text copyright © 1988 by Eloise Greenfield
Printed in the U.S.A. All rights reserved.
Typography by Harriett Barton
10 9 8 7 6 5 4 3 2 1
First Edition

Library of Congress Cataloging-in-Publication Data
Greenfield, Eloise.
    Under the Sunday tree : poems / by Eloise Greenfield ; paintings
by Amos Ferguson.—1st ed.
        p.   cm.
    Summary: A collection of poems and paintings that evoke life in the
Bahamas.
    ISBN 0-06-022254-9: $
    ISBN 0-06-022257-3 (lib. bdg.) : $
    1. Bahamas—Juvenile poetry.   2. Children's poetry, American.
[1. Bahamas—Poetry.   2. American poetry.]   I. Ferguson, Amos,
date, ill.   II. Title
PS3557.R39416U5 1988   87-29373
811'.54—dc19   CIP
                                                          AC

Under the Sunday Tree

That Kind of Day

It's that kind of day
and that kind of season
when the breeze is sweet
and the cool air calls
"Come out!"
It beckons the folks
who come out of doors
and wander about
pretending at first
to look for chores
although they know
they just want to walk
in the breeze and the pale
sunlight
it's that kind of day

To Catch a Fish

It takes more than a wish
to catch a fish
you take the hook
you add the bait
you concentrate
and then you wait
you wait   you wait
but not a bite
the fish don't have
an appetite
so tell them what
good bait you've got
and how your bait
can hit the spot
this works a whole
lot better than
a wish
if you really
want to catch
a fish

Gazebo

As always
after he feeds the animals
the boy will go
into the gazebo
and stand looking out
at the landscape
marveling that his
eyes can travel
such a long distance
while his feet
stand still

Song of the Water Lilies

Sing a song of colors
of soft petals in sunlight
sing a muted lilies song
music blooms in the
still waters

The Brave Ones

We hear the bell clanging

we come in a hurry

we come with our ladders and hoses

our hoses

we come in a hurry

to fight the fire

the furious fire

to smother the smoke

the smoke

we don't have much time

we climb, we spray

we are the brave ones who save

who save

we are the brave ones who save

Her Dreams

In her dreams
there are sometimes trees
on which hang ornaments
as tall as she
she lifts her arms
to touch them
if she can stretch
high enough to
claim them
they will become
the jewelled moments
of her life.

When the Tourists Come to Town

When the tourists come to town
they fill the streets with noise
and bustling fun
fill the carriages and sidewalks
some, pretending they are queens
leaning looking silly as they ride
when the tourists come to town
their worries cast aside
they shop
fill their bags with fascinating stuff
fill their lives with warmth and sun
enough to carry home for winter
when their trip is done

PAINTED BY MR
AMOS. FERGUSON

Thoughts

I stand in the center
and make the traffic flow
for people whose names
I don't even know

Who are these people
I never meet
where are they going
and what do they do
when they're not riding
down my street?

The Tree

It graces our yard
bears beauty and fruit
we breathe deeply
the sight of it
the scent of it
we touch it gently

Saucer-Hat Lady

Look at that!
look at that lady
in the saucer hat
don't she look pretty
I'm telling you
betcha anything
that she knows it, too
don't nobody try
to tell her that
she ain't looking sassy
in her saucer hat

The Sailboat Race

The boats are ready

to race

each wants to sail

at the fastest pace

they're ready to ride

the water's wings

and listen as the wind sings

a tale of those who have

sailed before

the boats are ready

to soar

to turn their sails

against the air

that pushes them

from here to there

they hear the signal

to start the chase

to see who will win

in the sailboat race

and they're off!

Tradition

Pineapples! pumpkins! chickens! we
carry them on our heads you see
we can glide along forever
and not drop a thing, no never
never even use our hands
never put a finger to it
you know how we learned to do it?
knowledge came from other lands
Africans of long ago
passed it down to us and so
now we pass it on to you
for what is old is also new
pineapples, pumpkins, chickens, we
carry more than the things you see
we also carry history

THE PINE APPLE WOMEN
PAINT BY MR AMOS
FERGUSON 1786

THE PUMPKIN
MAN

THE CHICKEN
WOMEN

This Place

There is this place I know
where children go to find
their deepest feelings
they look behind the trees
for hiding wants and angers
bashful joys
this place is quiet
no shouts may enter
no rolling laughter
but only silent tears
to carry the feelings
forward in waves
that wash the children
whole

PAINT BY MR AMOS FERGUSON 1984

Wedding Day

The sun shone too hot
the veil wouldn't stay
the pianist never
came to play
but love is what made it
a perfect day

The Man in Red

Whenever he
puts on his
red jacket
red tie and
his serious face
to match
the neighbors know he's
going someplace
special

Lucky Little Birds

They're lucky little birds
they don't have to hear
their parents over and over again
say, "Chew your food, now, dear."

They never have to try
to turn their food into pulp
they only have to open their mouths
and gulp

Under the Sunday Tree

They walk together
on Sundays
move slowly
through the park
always remembering
to stop awhile
at the place where
two trees arch as one
leaves touching
like family

Donkey

Oh, he likes us, he's our friend
that's why he lets us pretend
we're going for a donkey ride
but all the time he knows inside
that he's not going anywhere
he's just going to stand right there
he says as much in donkey talk,
"Hee-haw, when you get down, I'll walk.
I don't take passengers or freight,
I only carry my own weight."
Still we like to play this game
and we love him just the same
even though he'll stand right there
and never take us anywhere

Buddies

A boy and a bird can be buddies

not the kind who run

in the sunshine together

or gather for games of sport

but buddies of another sort

who meet just at mealtimes maybe

and trust

To Friendship

It's time for the party
and as we begin
let's do a sentimental
thing
let's lift our punch
to the bunch
(that's us)
we'll say that our
friendship is dear and
we'll promise to keep it from
year to year
and
this toast we'll repeat
each time we meet
and now, my friends—
let's eat